MW00353244

Where the Wildflowers Grow

by

Adriana Picker

A gentle breeze ripples through fields of glorious green and red. Rose and alabaster lillies move with the gentle current of a secret rainforest brook. Dappled sunshine warms your face and captures the riotous golden blossoms above your head.

Take your time to colour in every detail of natural beauty and let Adriana Picker's intricate illustrations transport you to a mesmerising hidden world where wildflowers bloom at your feet and birdsong rings in your ears.

Adriana Picker is an illustrator based in Sydney, Australia. At the heart of Adriana's work is a lifelong passion for botanical illustration. *Where the Wildflowers Grow* is an expression of her love for Australian flora and fauna.

Her first colouring book for adults is *The Garden of Earthly Delights*.

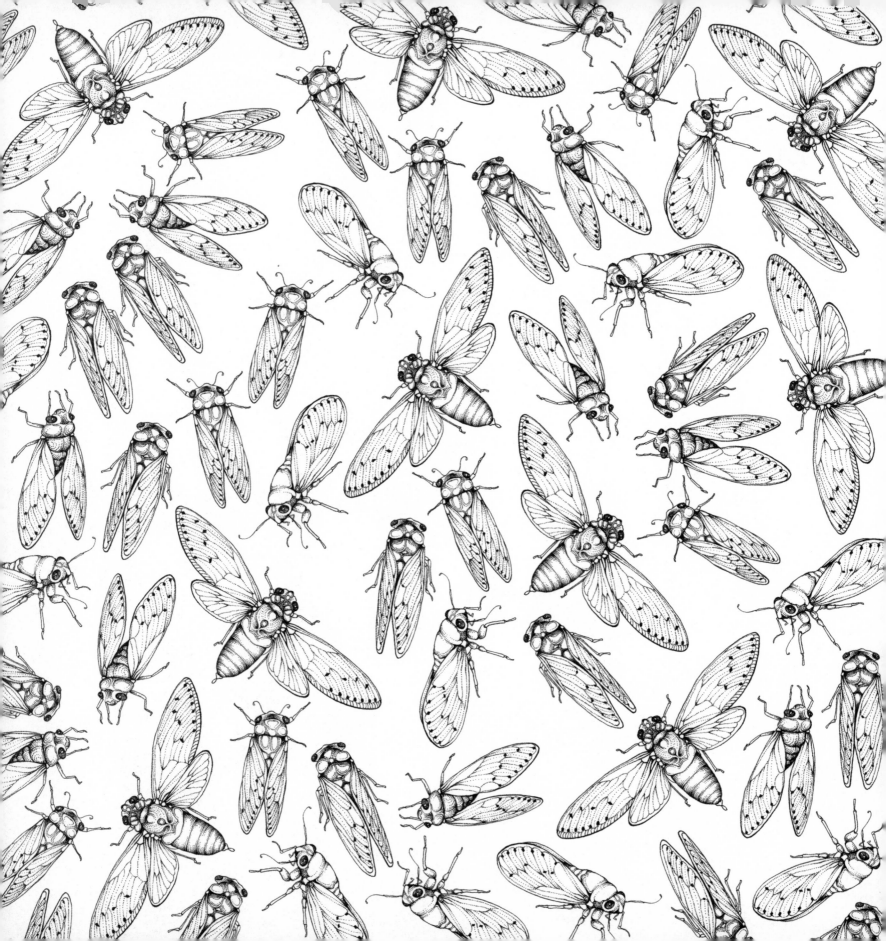

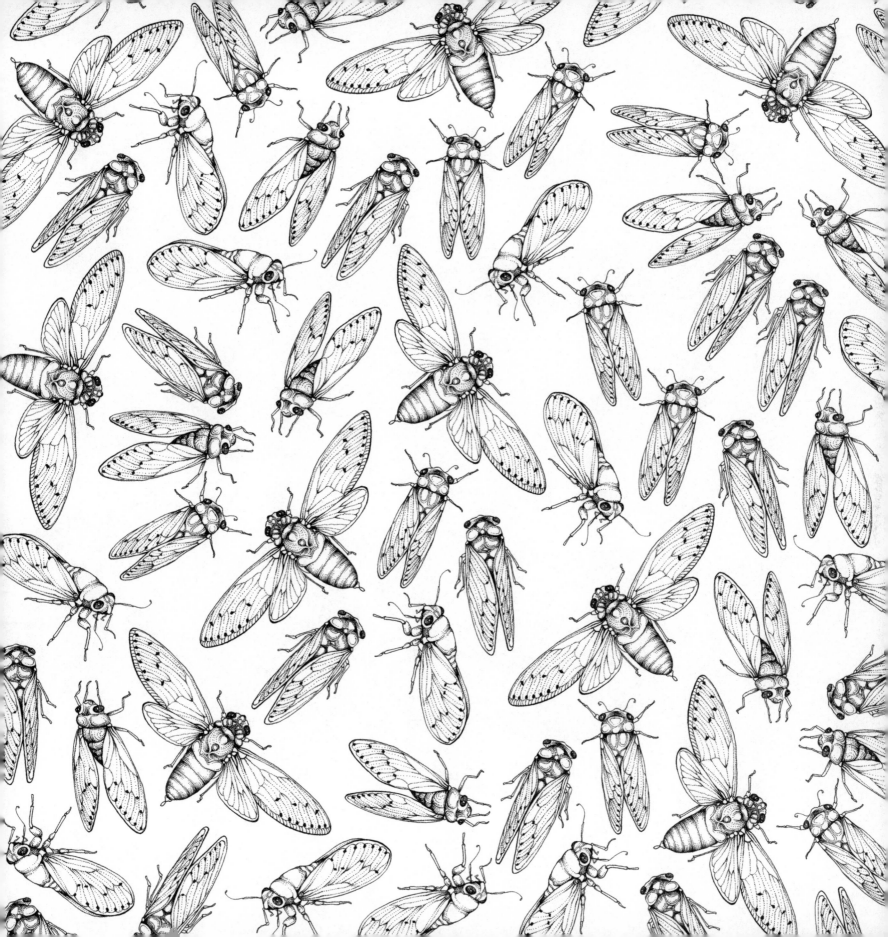

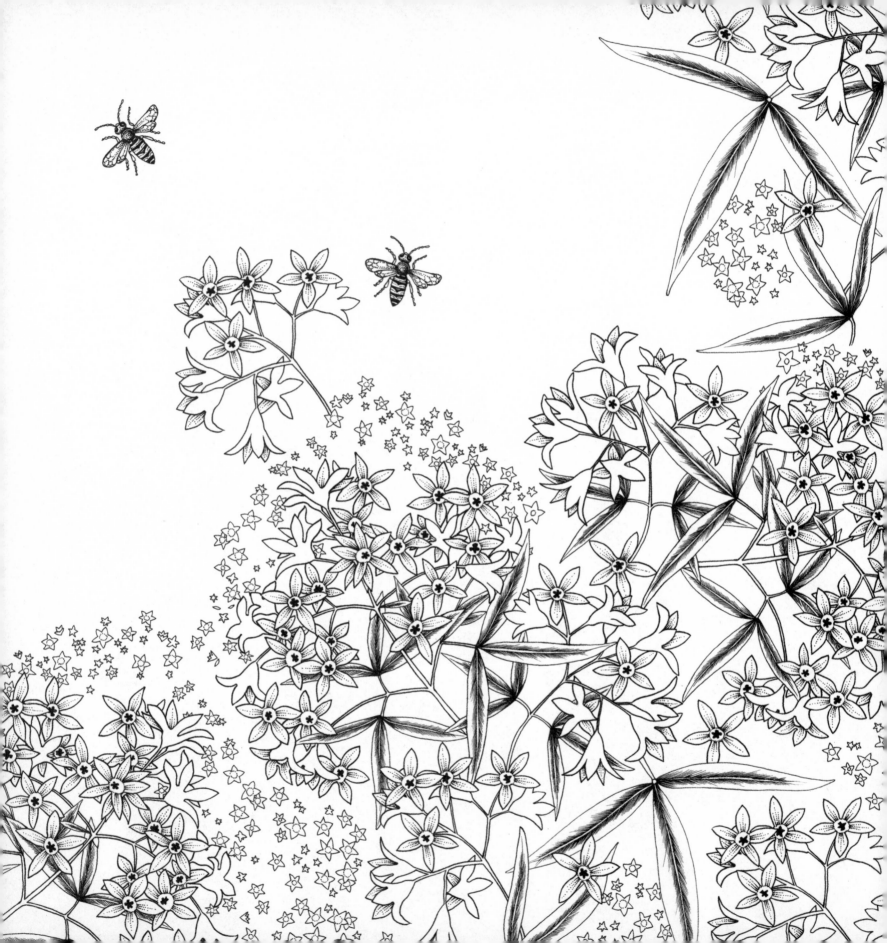

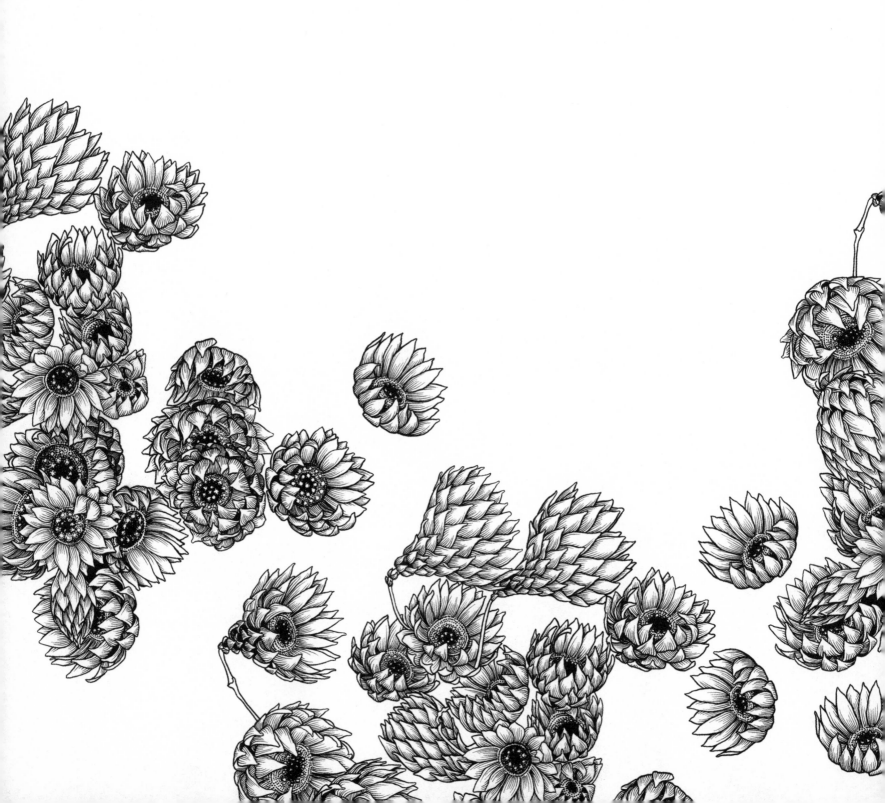

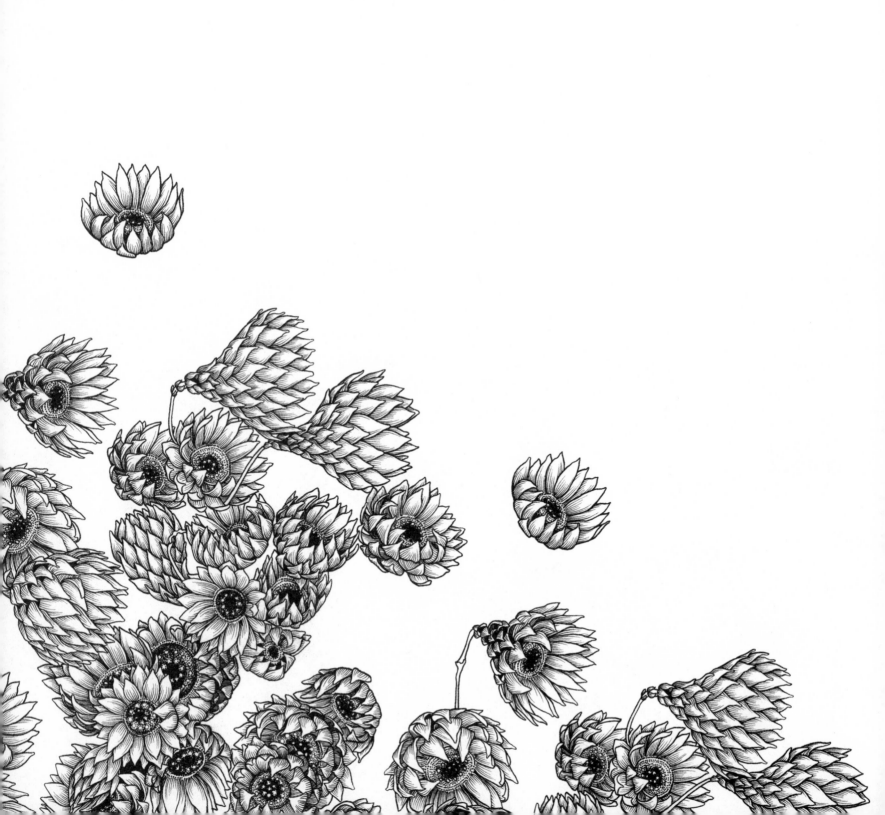

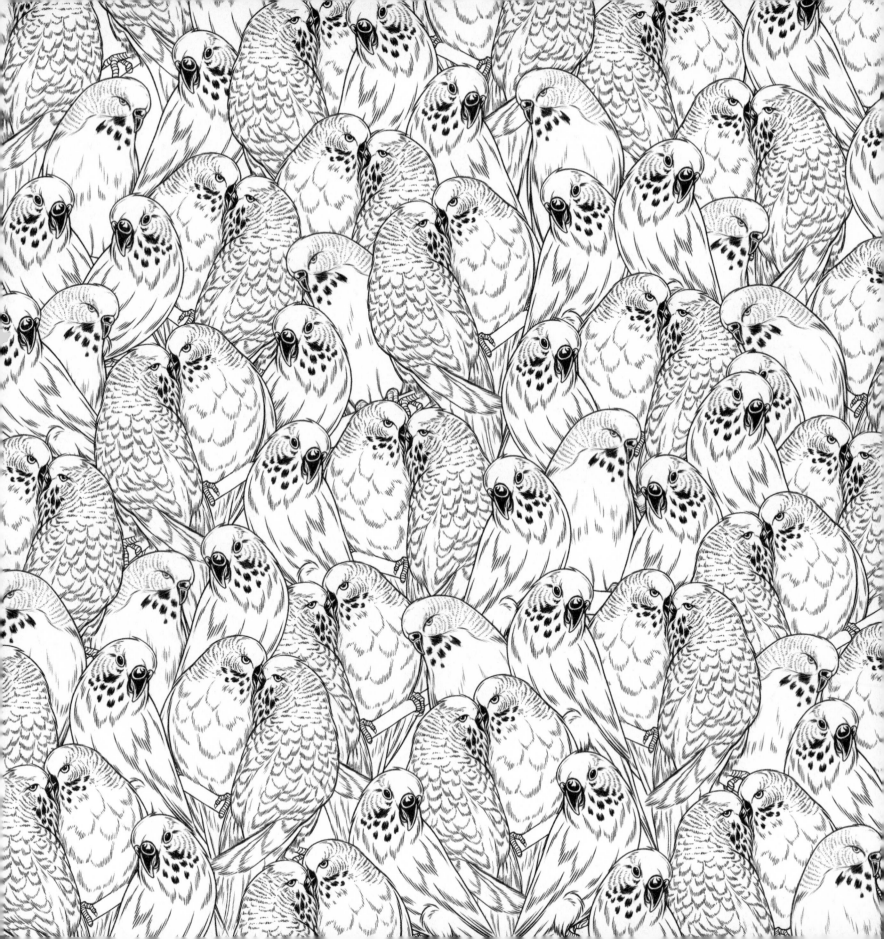

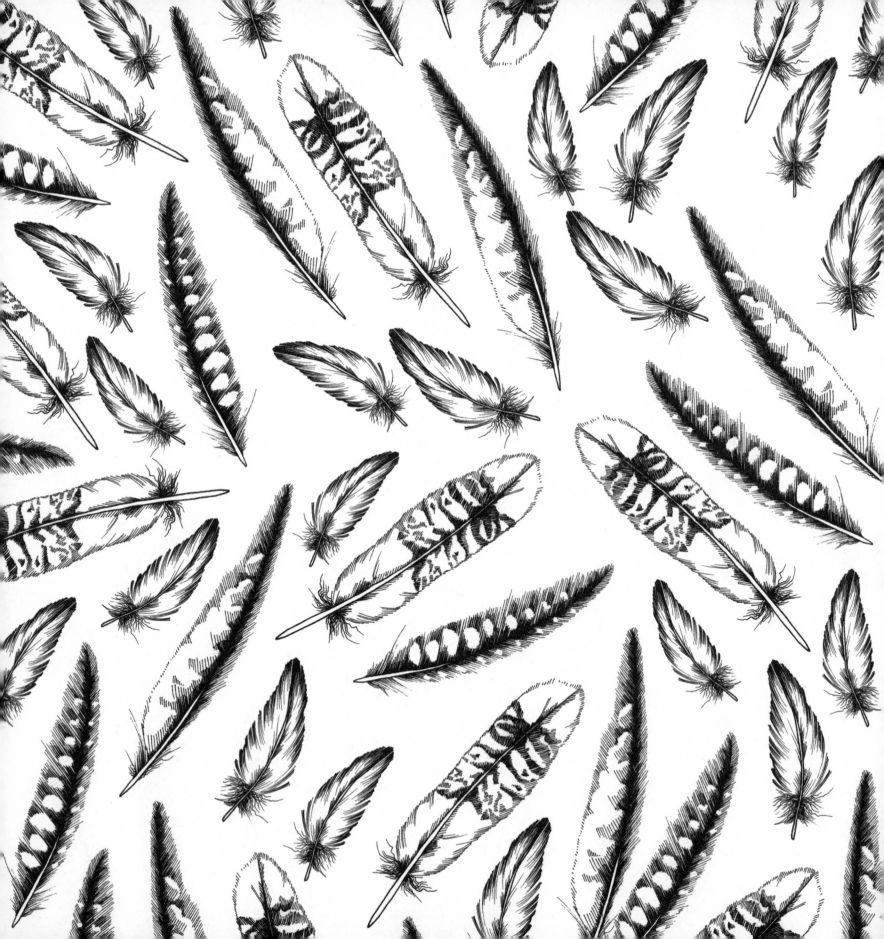

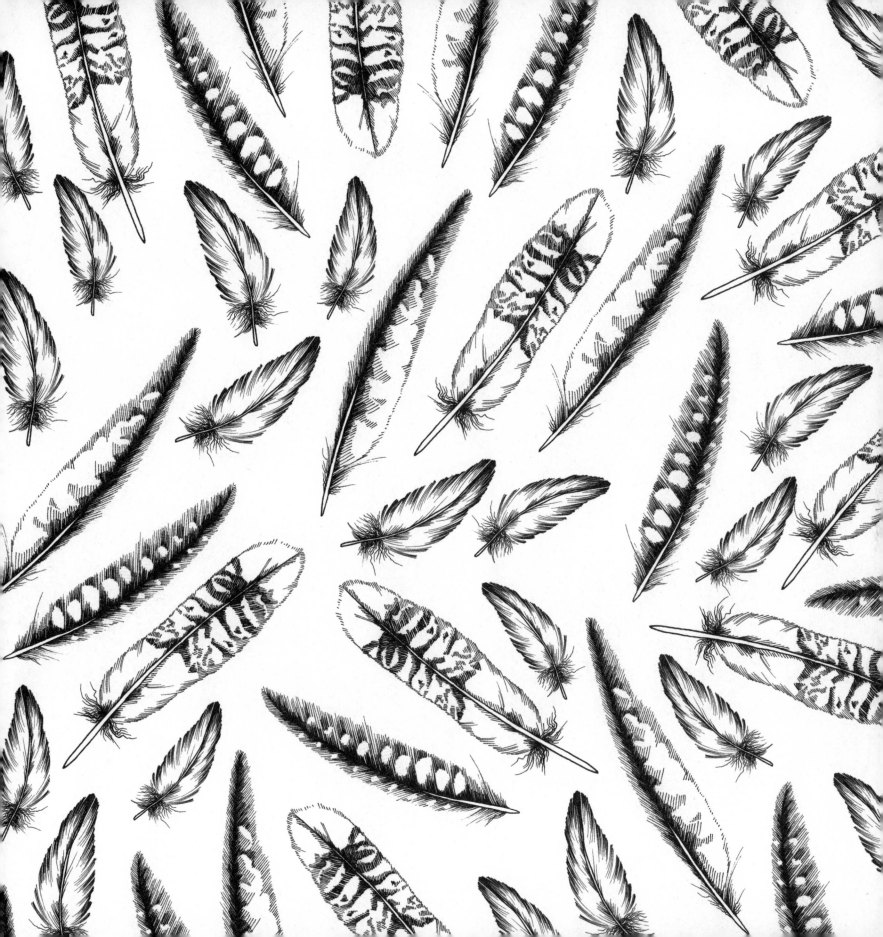

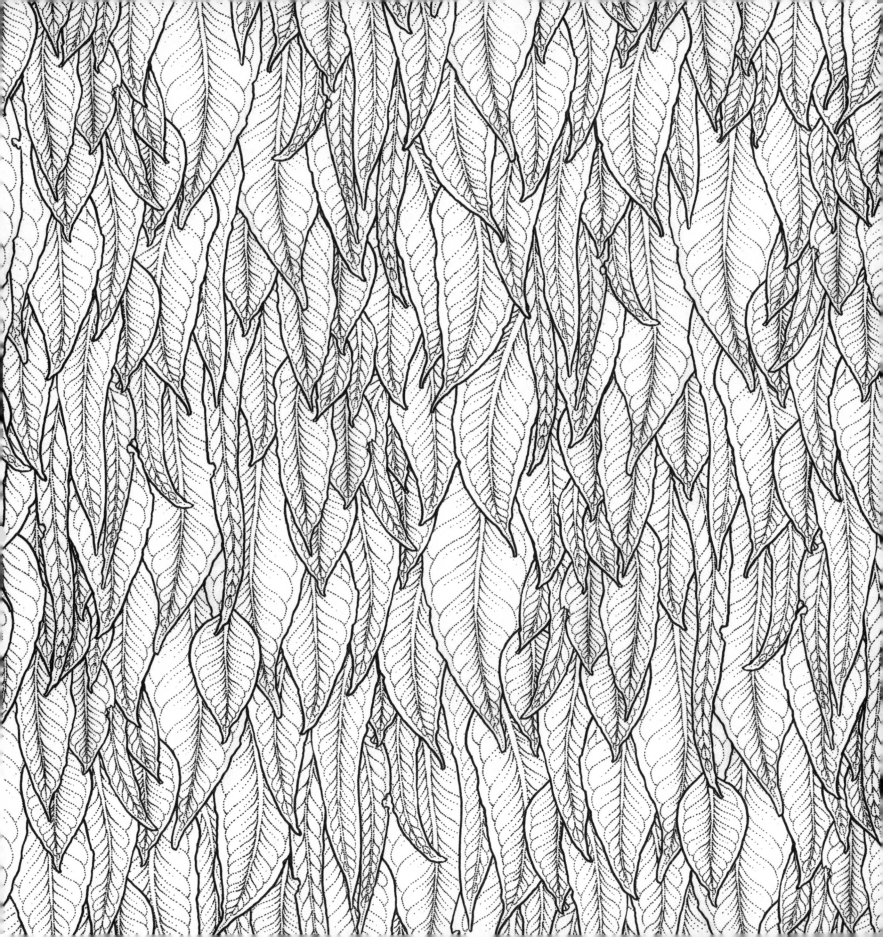

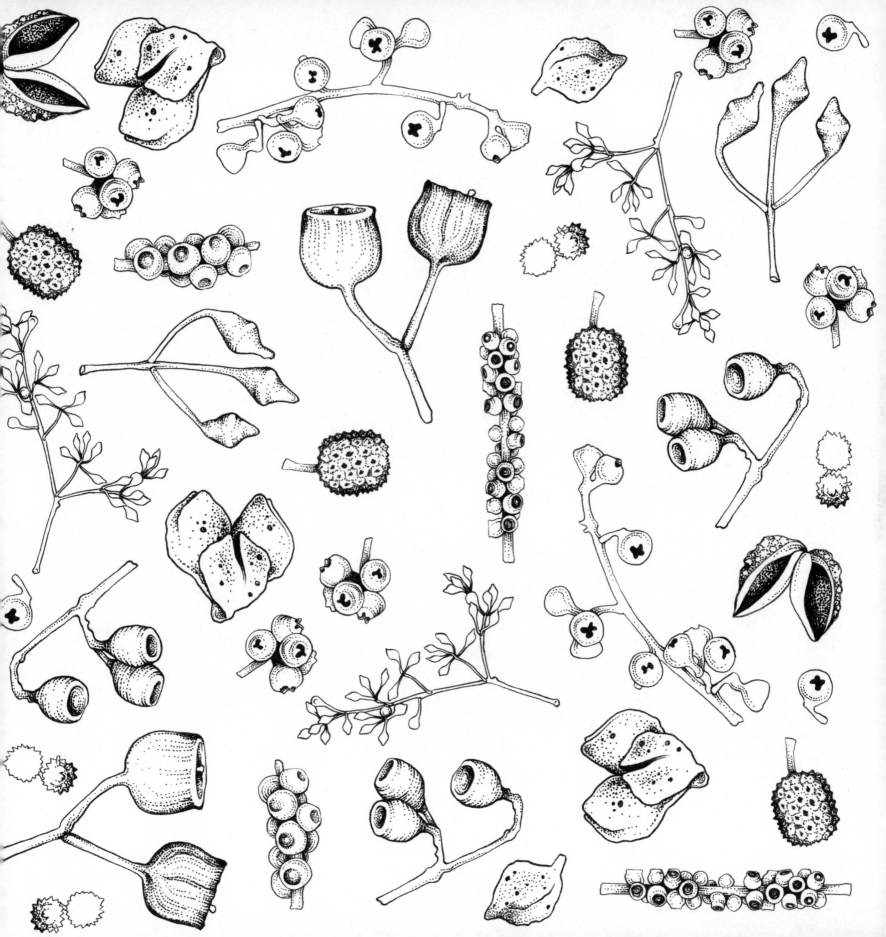

Published in 2016 by Hardie Grant Books

Hardie Grant Books (Australia)
Ground Floor, Building 1
658 Church Street
Richmond, Victoria 3121
www.hardiegrant.com.au

Hardie Grant Books (UK)
5th & 6th Floors
52–54 Southwark Street
London SE1 1UN
www.hardiegrant.co.uk

All rights reserved. No part of this publication may be reproduced, stored in a retrieval system or transmitted in
any form by any means, electronic, mechanical, photocopying, recording or otherwise, without the prior written
permission of the publishers and copyright holders.

The moral rights of the author have been asserted.

Copyright text © Adriana Picker 2016
Copyright illustrations © Adriana Picker 2016
Copyright design © Hardie Grant Books 2016

A Cataloguing-in-Publication entry is available from the catalogue of the National Library of Australia
at www.nla.gov.au

Where the Wildflowers Grow
ISBN 978 1 74379 170 7
US ISBN 978 1 74379 190 5

Publishing Director: Fran Berry
Project Editors: Rachel Day and Rihana Ries
Design Manager: Mark Campbell
Production Manager: Todd Rechner

Printed in China by Leo Paper Products LTD.

FSC
www.fsc.org
MIX
Paper from
responsible sources
FSC® C020056

The paper this book is printed on is from FSC®-certified
forests and other sources. FSC® promotes environmentally
responsible, socially beneficial and economically viable
management of the world's forests.